STEPS FOR
DRAWING ANIMALS
ACTIVITY BOOK

Bobo's Children Activity Books

BOBO's
CHILDREN ACTIVITY BOOKS
COLORING, DRAWING & ACTIVITY BOOKS FOR CHILDREN

Copyright 2016

INSTRUCTIONS FOR DRAWING:

THIS HOW-TO DRAWING BOOK CONSISTS OF IMAGES THAT ARE PLACED ON GRIDS. THERE IS AN EMPTY DRAWING BOX WITH GRIDS THAT WILL SERVE AS YOUR PRACTICE SPACE. TO COPY EACH IMAGE, DRAW PARTS OF THE IMAGE PER GRID AND PUT THEM ON THE BLANK GRIDS. SOUNDS DIFFICULT? NOT REALLY. TRY IT FIRST!

IT'S OKAY IF YOU DON'T COPY THE IMAGE PERFECTLY. AFTER ALL, DRAWING IS ABOUT THE EXPRESSION OF YOUR PERCEPTION AS WELL AS YOUR HAND STRENGTH AND CONTROL.

WHEN YOU'VE COPIED THE IMAGE, GO AHEAD AND COLOR IT NEXT! WE'RE EXCITED TO SEE WHAT YOU CAN DO!

DRAW
THE
IMAGE

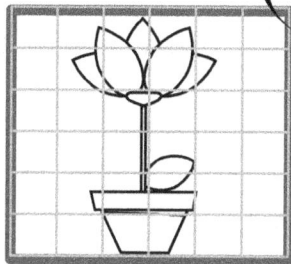

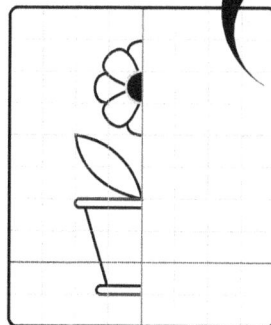

Draw the animals with the easy guides.

DRAW
THE
IMAGE

This is a Drawing Page
Find Other Great Titles By searching for BoBo's Children Activity Books on Your Favorite Book Retailer
Amazon.Com | Barnes & Noble (BN.Com) | Books A Million (BAM.Com)

Draw the animals with the easy guides.

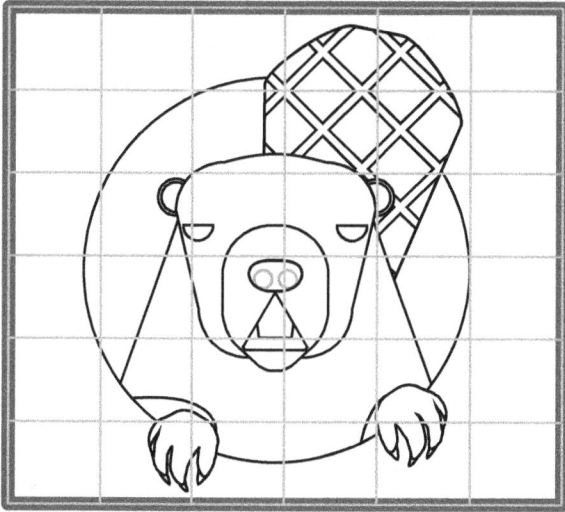

DRAW
THE
IMAGE

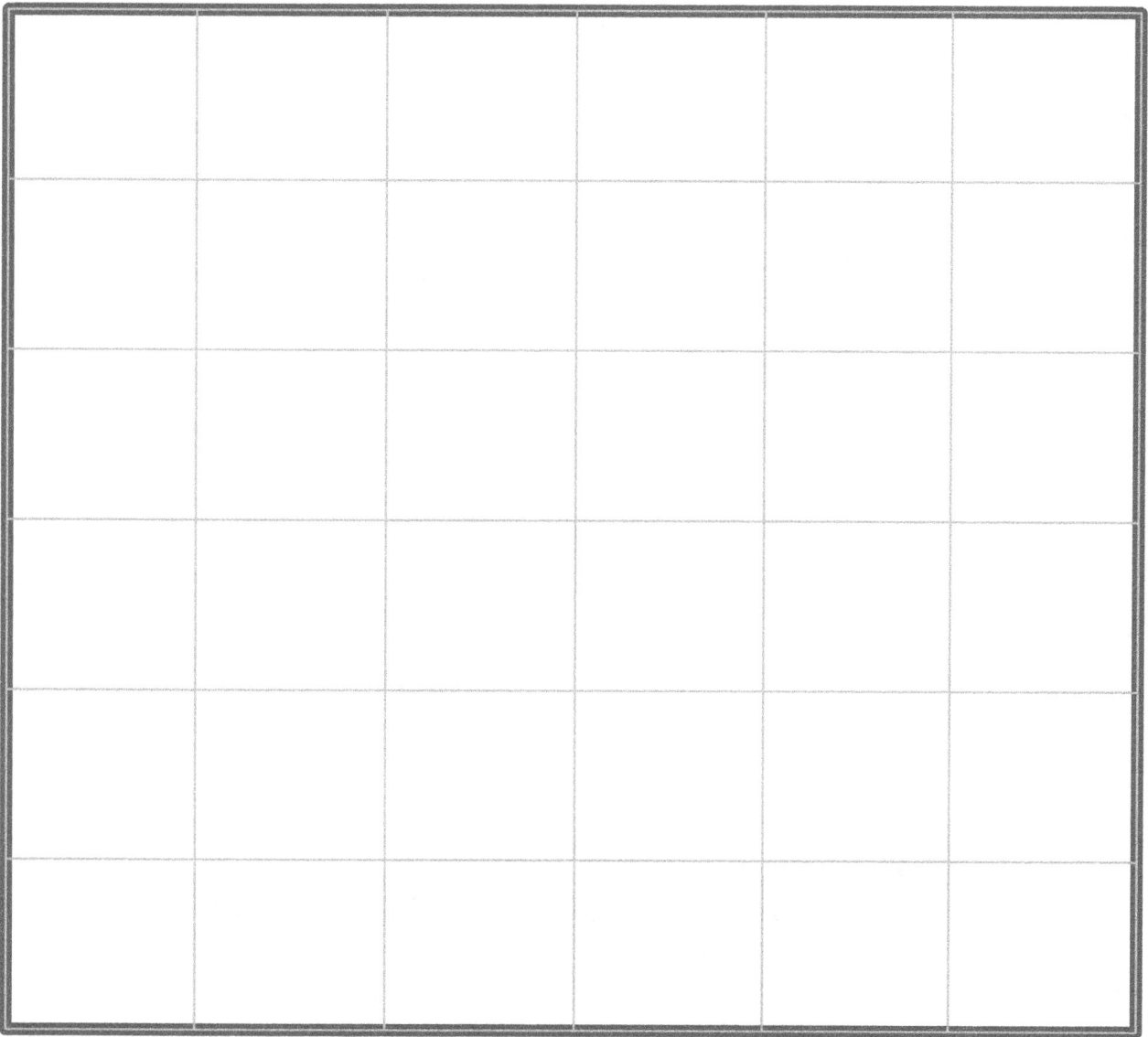

This is a Drawing Page

Find Other Great Titles By searching for BoBo's Children Activity Books on Your Favorite Book Retailer

Amazon.Com | Barnes & Noble (BN.Com) | Books A Million (BAM.Com)

Draw the animals with the easy guides.

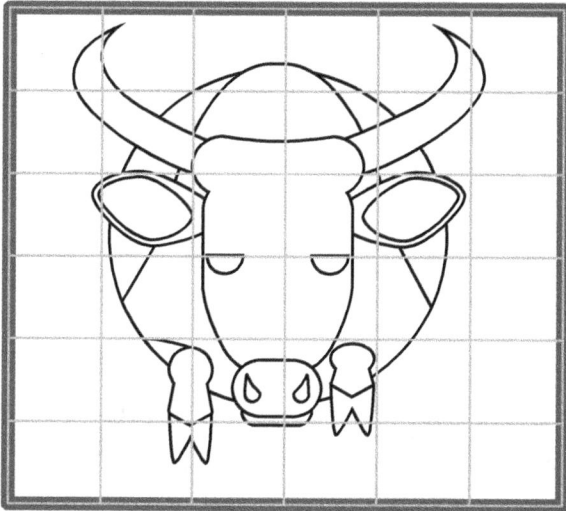

DRAW
THE
IMAGE

Draw the animals with the easy guides.

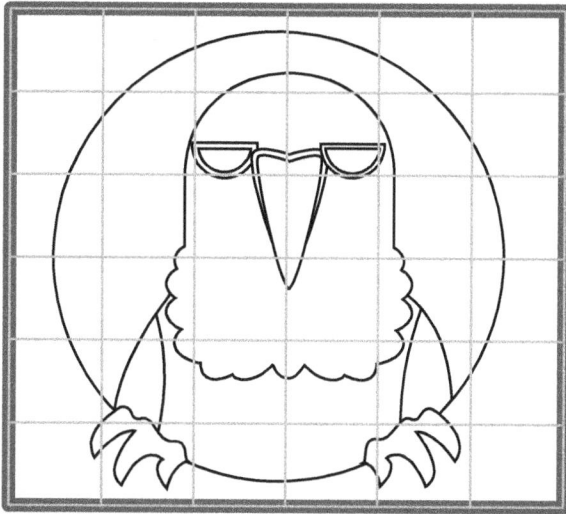

DRAW
THE
IMAGE

Draw the animals with the easy guides.

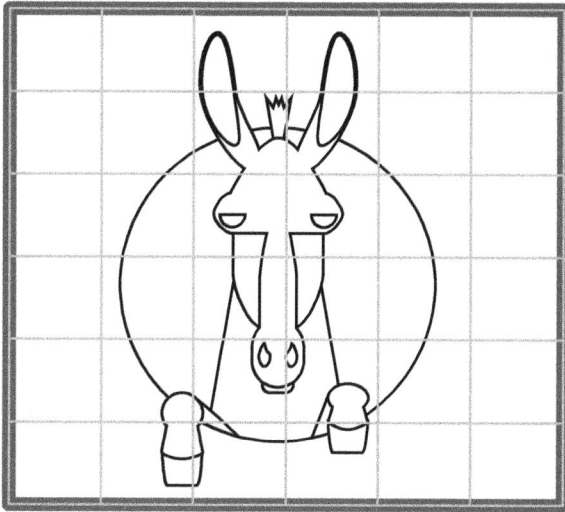

DRAW
THE
IMAGE

Draw the animals with the easy guides.

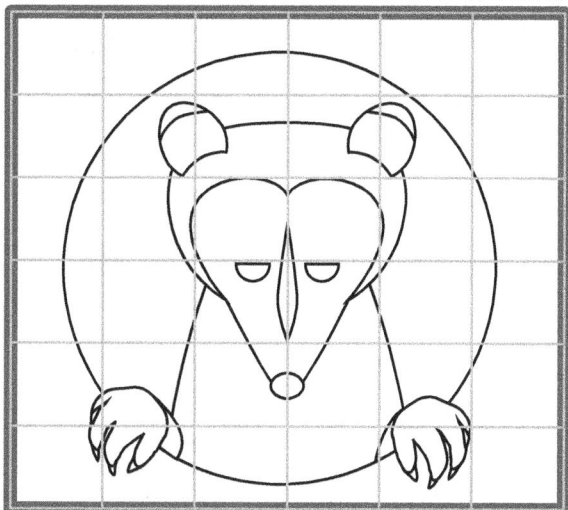

DRAW
THE
IMAGE

Draw the animals with the easy guides.

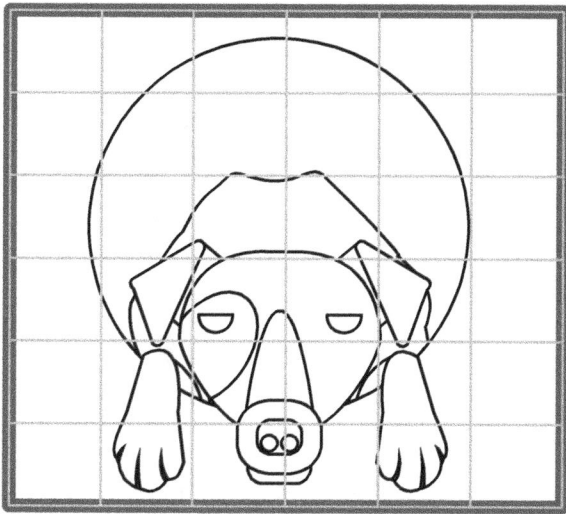

DRAW
THE
IMAGE

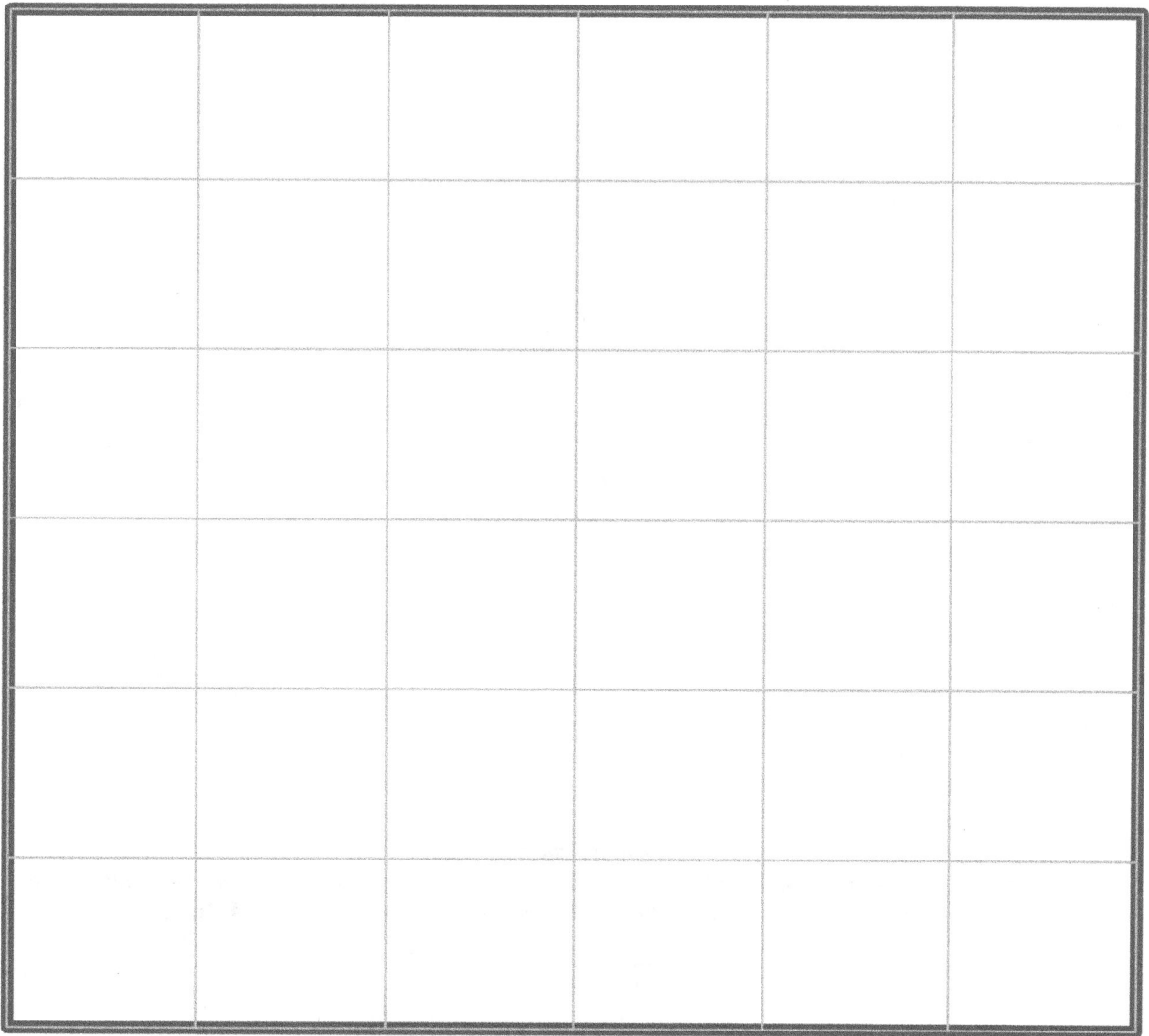

Draw the animals with the easy guides.

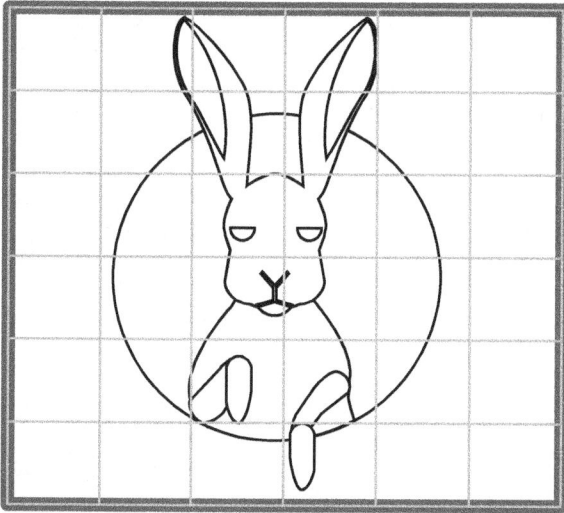

DRAW
THE
IMAGE

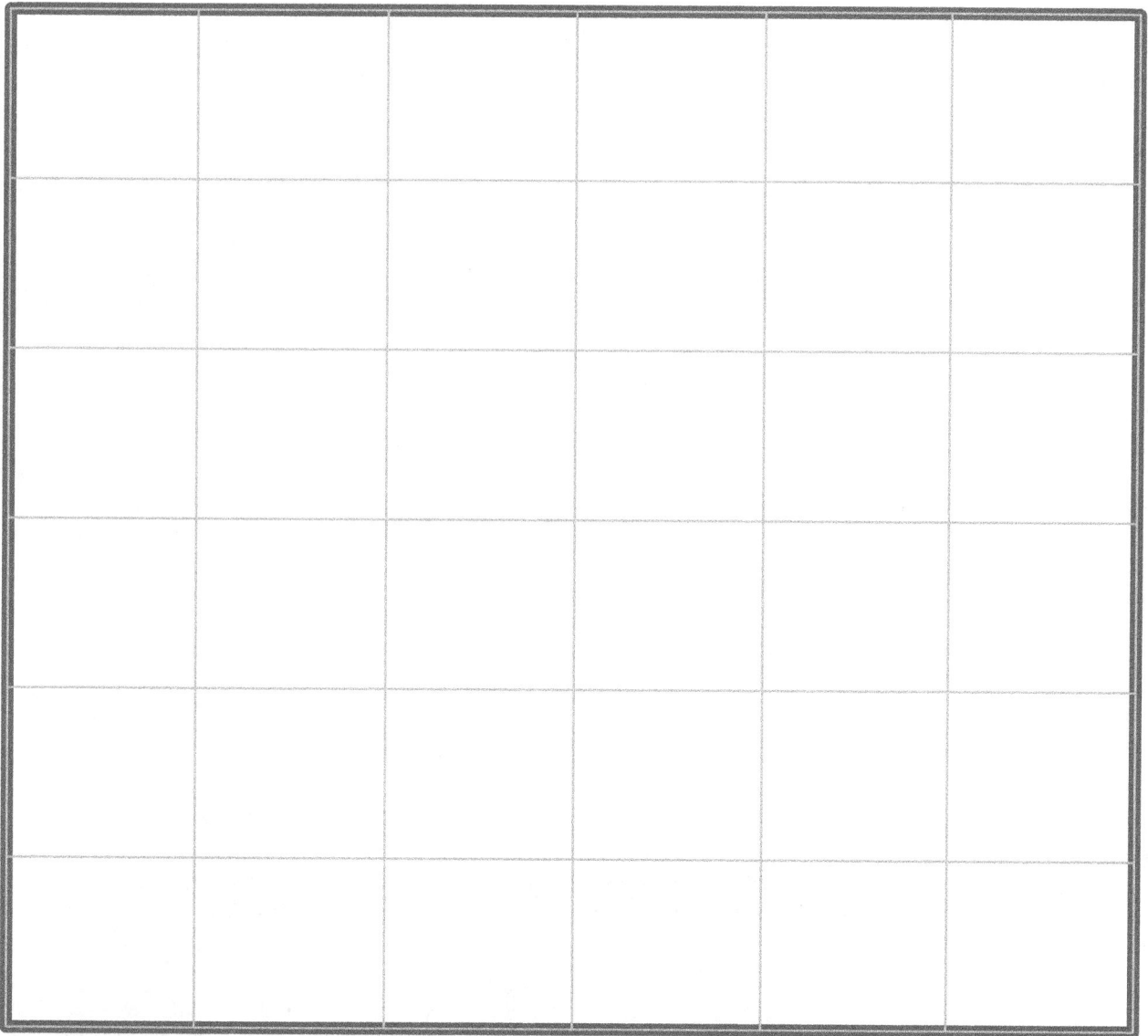

This is a Drawing Page

Find Other Great Titles By searching for BoBo's Children Activity Books on Your Favorite Book Retailer

Amazon.Com | Barnes & Noble (BN.Com) | Books A Million (BAM.Com)

Draw the animals with the easy guides.

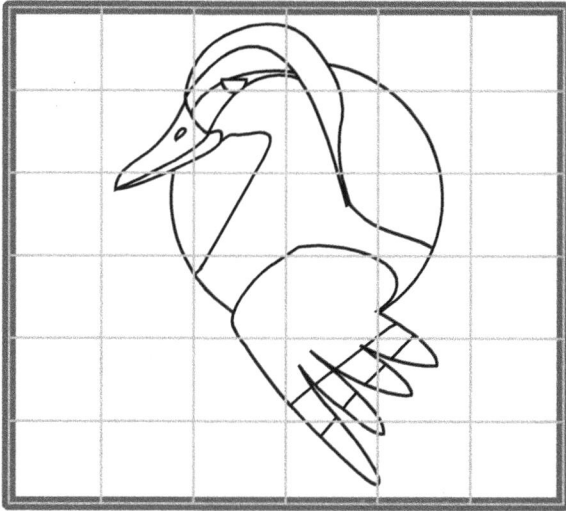

DRAW
THE
IMAGE

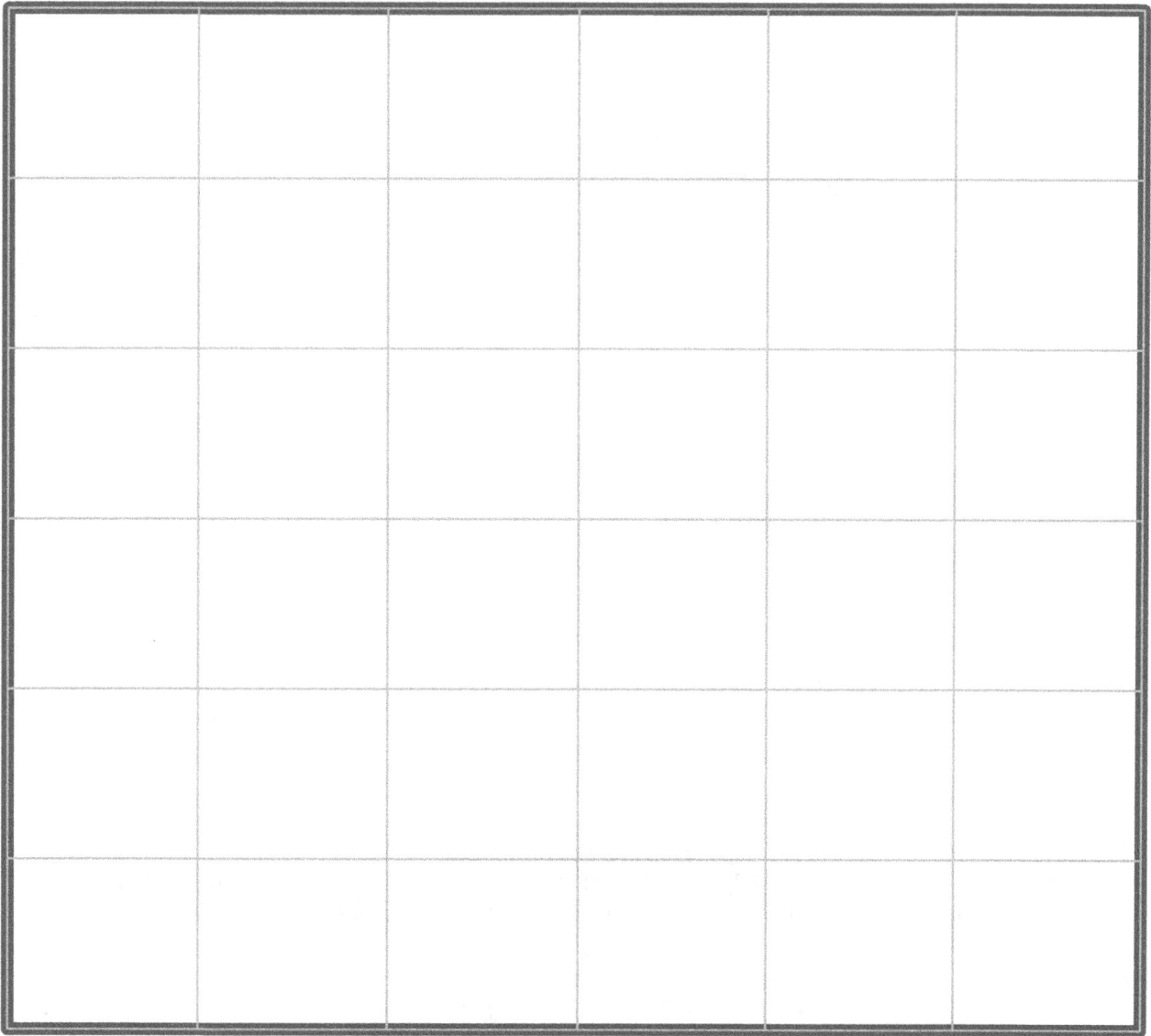

This is a Drawing Page
Find Other Great Titles By searching for BoBo's Children Activity Books on Your Favorite Book Retailer
Amazon.Com | Barnes & Noble (BN.Com) | Books A Million (BAM.Com)

Draw the animals with the easy guides.

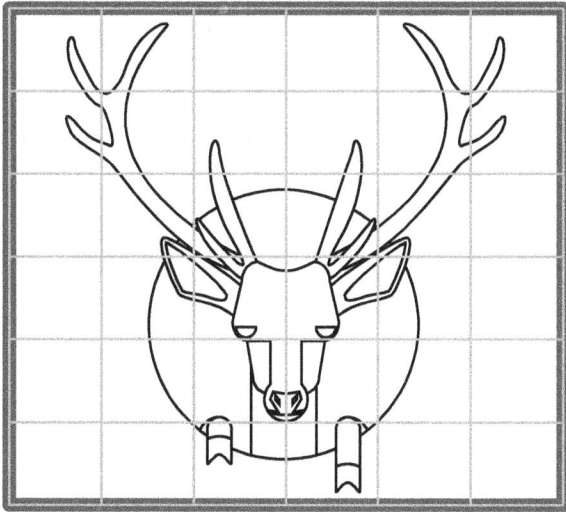

DRAW
THE
IMAGE

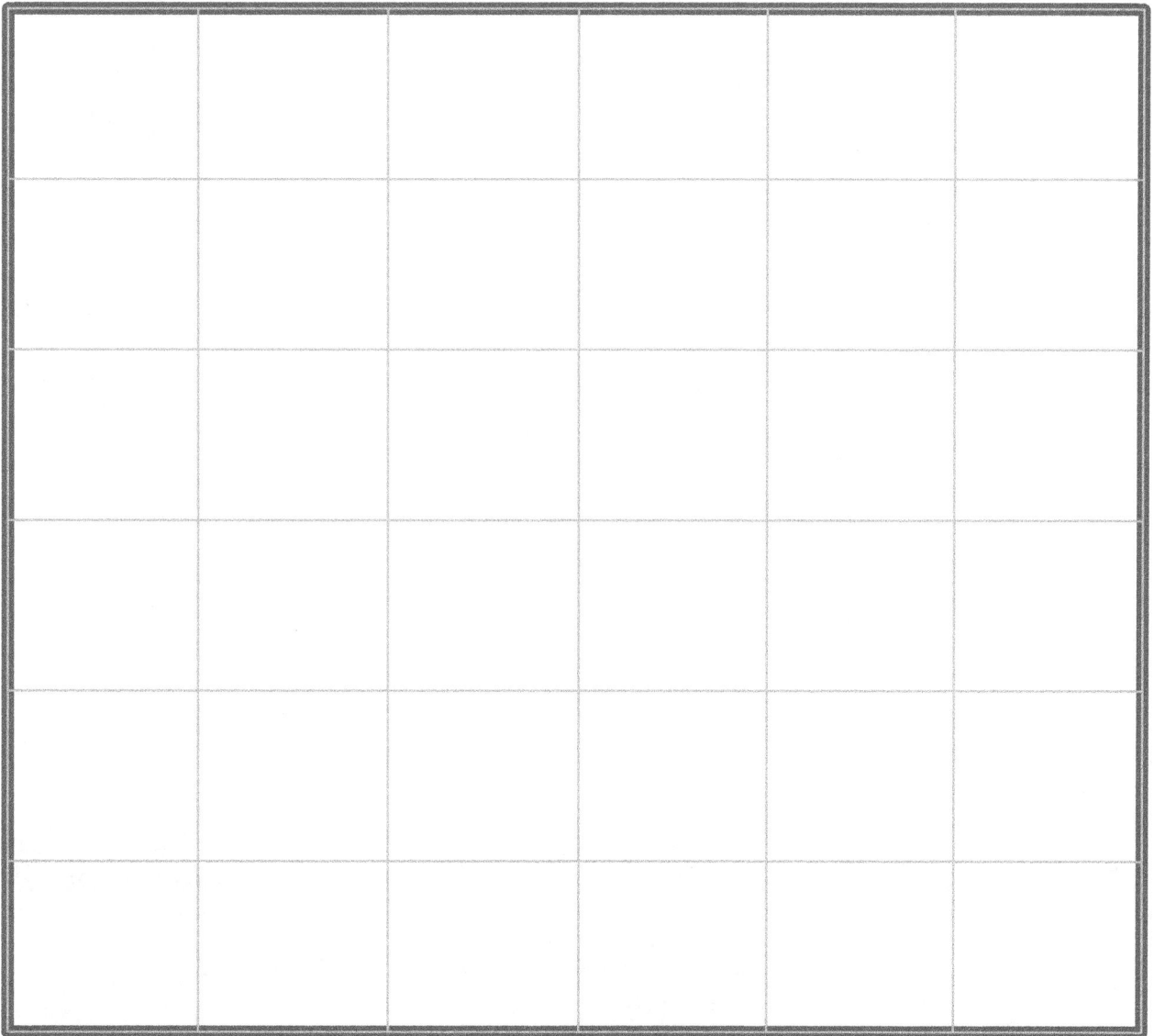

Draw the animals with the easy guides.

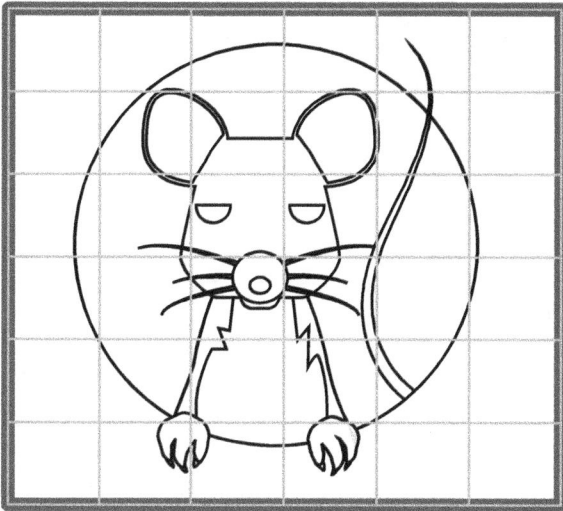

DRAW
THE
IMAGE

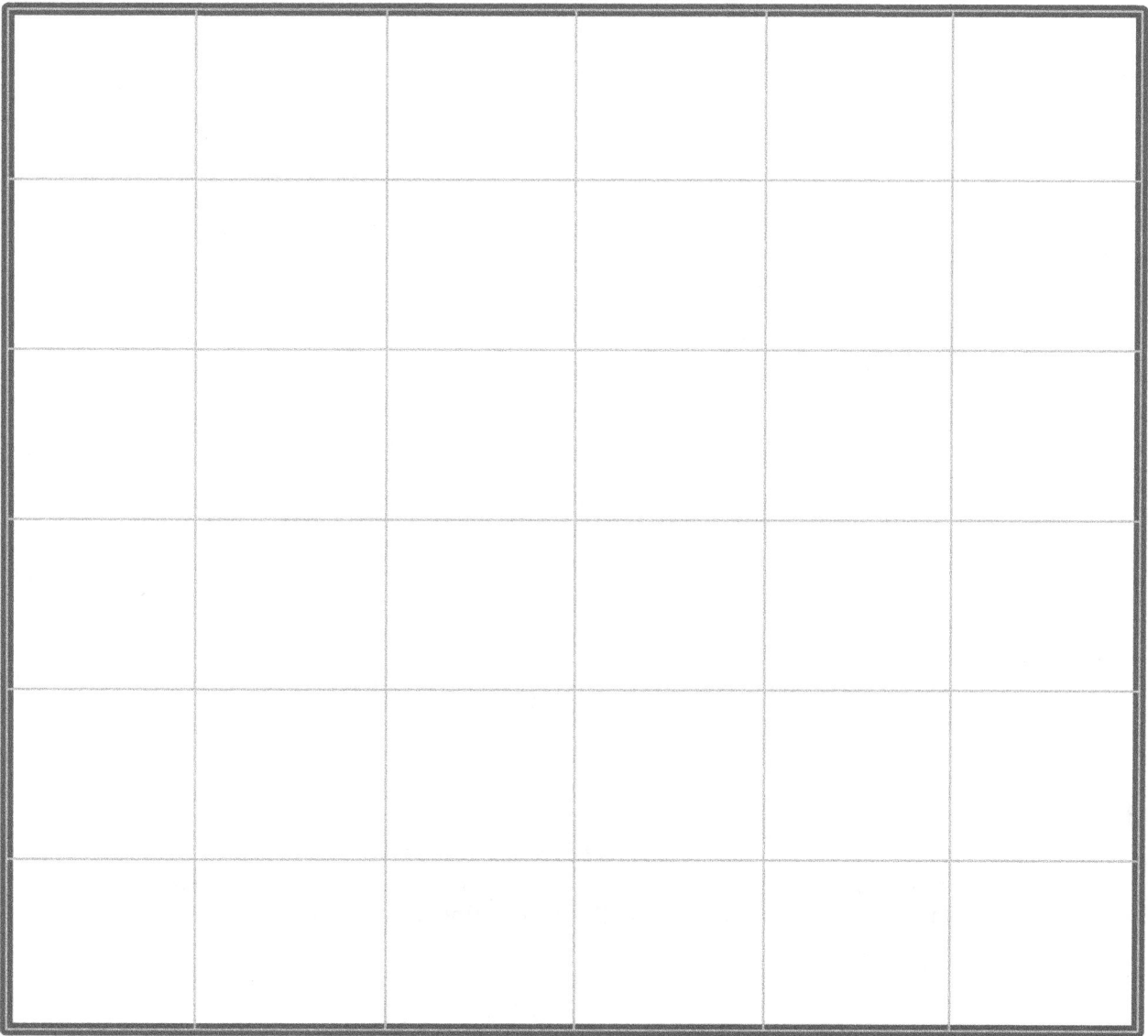

Draw the animals with the easy guides.

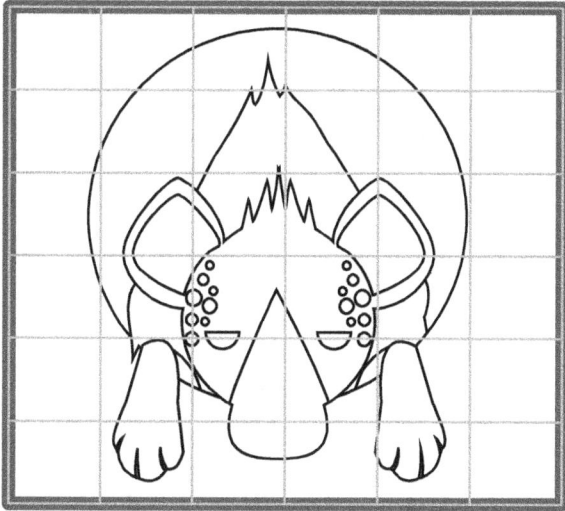

DRAW
THE
IMAGE

DRAW
THE
IMAGE

This is a Drawing Page
Find Other Great Titles By searching for BoBo's Children Activity Books on Your Favorite Book Retailer
Amazon.Com | Barnes & Noble (BN.Com) | Books A Million (BAM.Com)

Draw the animals with the easy guides.

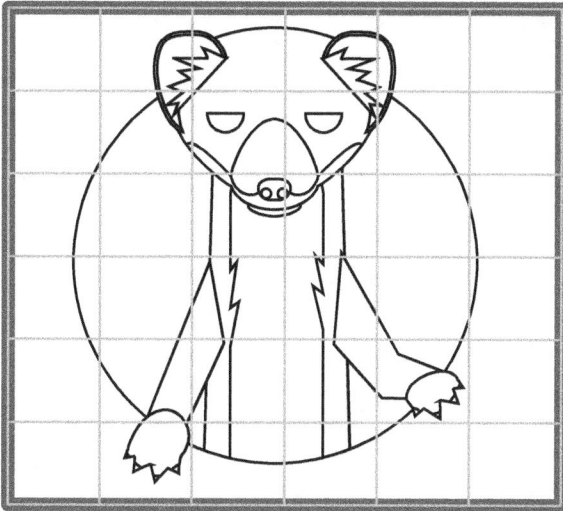

DRAW
THE
IMAGE

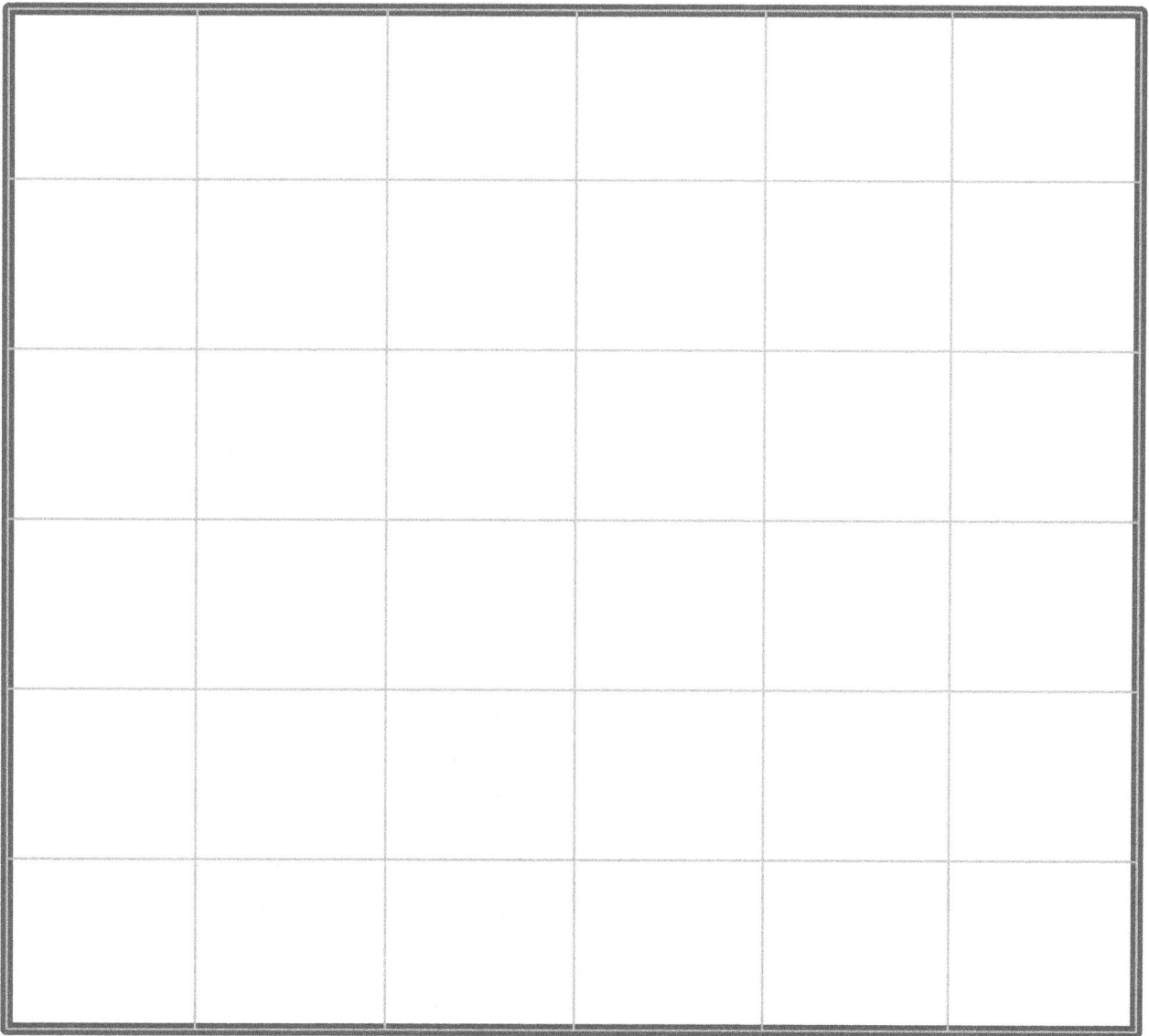

Draw the animals with the easy guides.

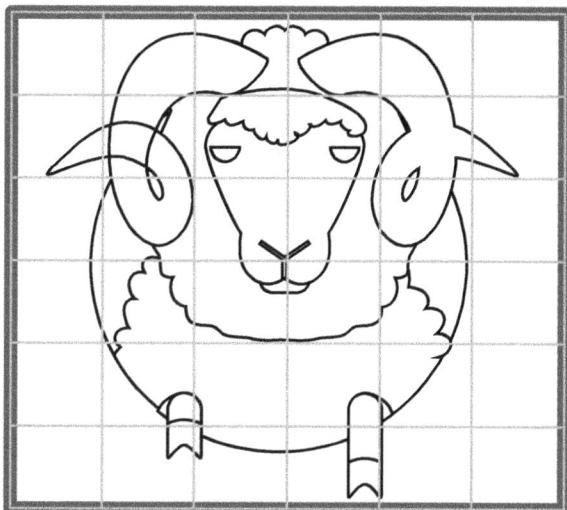

DRAW
THE
IMAGE

This is a Drawing Page

Find Other Great Titles By searching for BoBo's Children Activity Books on Your Favorite Book Retailer

Amazon.Com | Barnes & Noble (BN.Com) | Books A Million (BAM.Com)

BOBO's

CHILDREN ACTIVITY BOOKS

COLORING, DRAWING & ACTIVITY BOOKS FOR CHILDREN

Draw the animals with the easy guides.

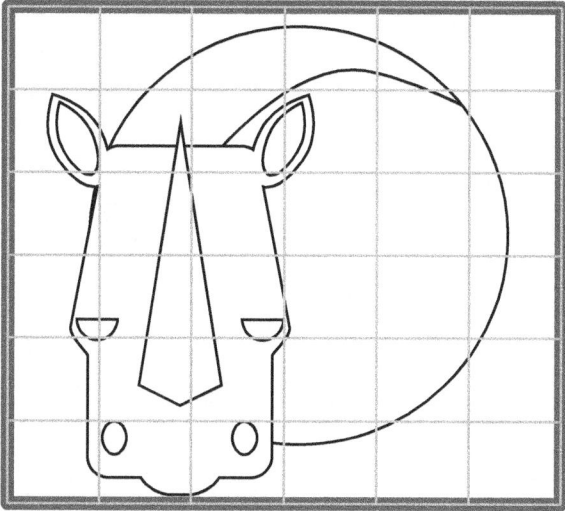

DRAW
THE
IMAGE

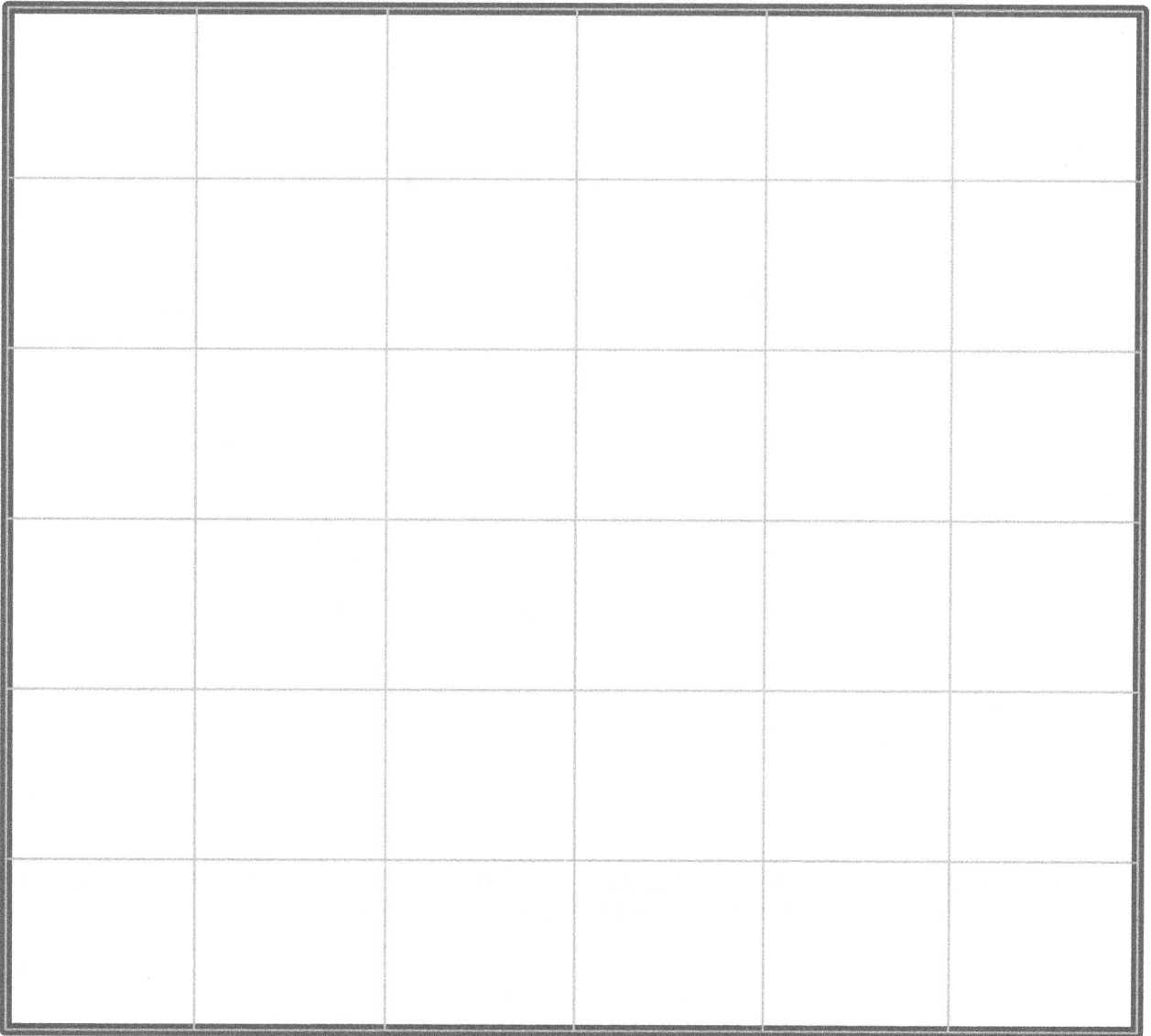

This is a Drawing Page
Find Other Great Titles By searching for BoBo's Children Activity Books on Your Favorite Book Retailer
Amazon.Com | Barnes & Noble (BN.Com) | Books A Million (BAM.Com)

Draw the animals with the easy guides.

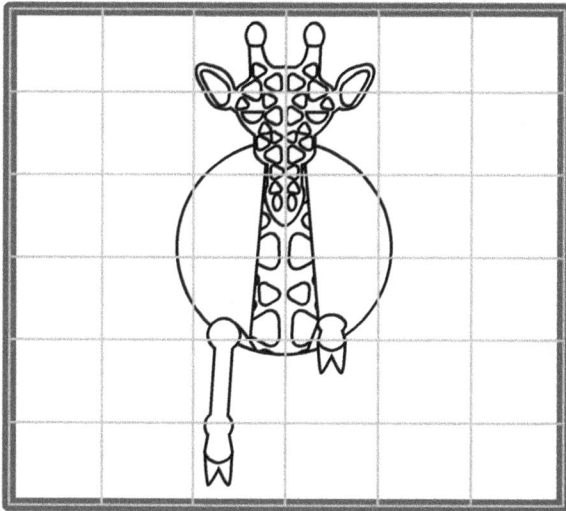

DRAW
THE
IMAGE

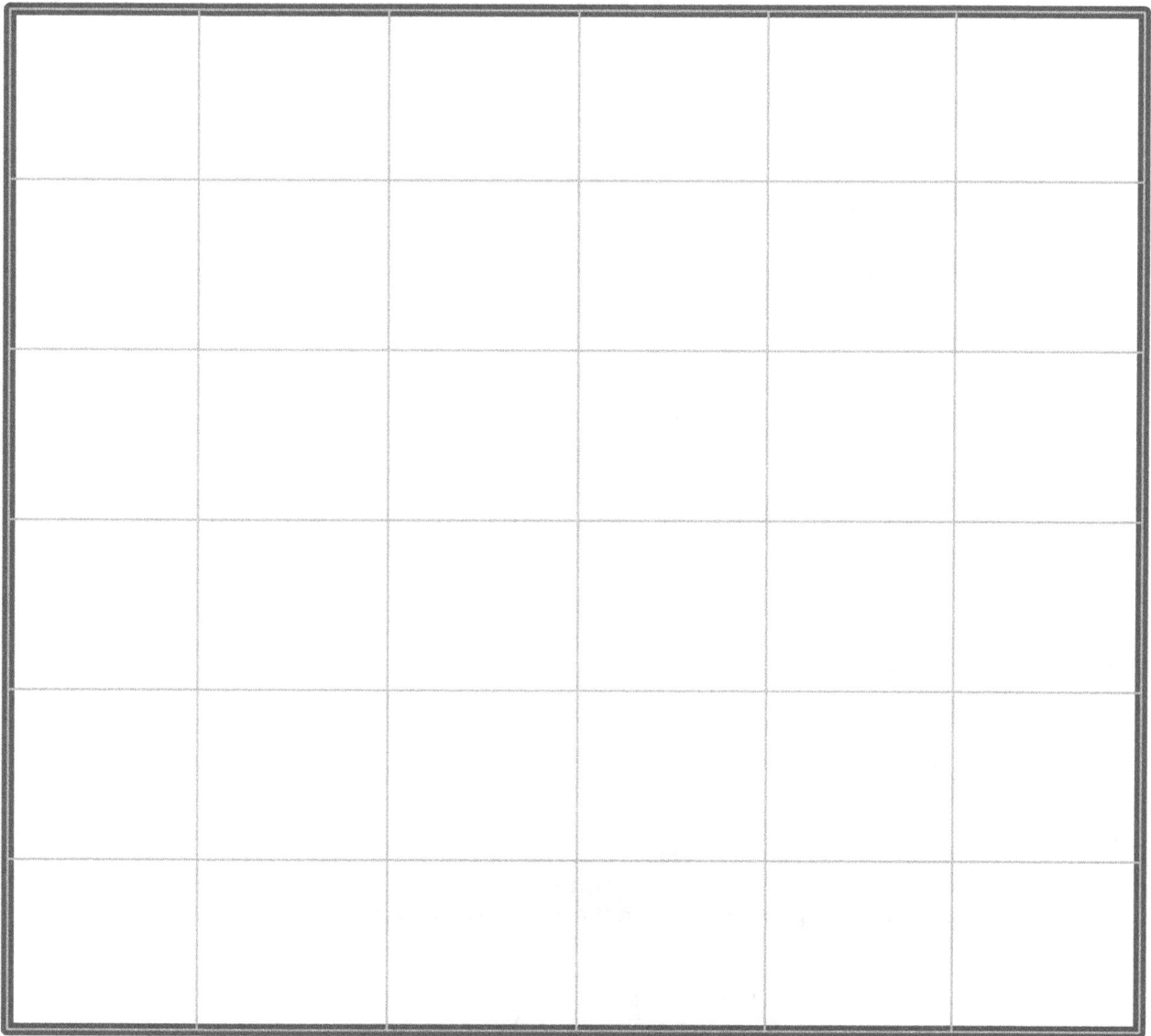

This is a Drawing Page

Find Other Great Titles By searching for BoBo's Children Activity Books on Your Favorite Book Retailer

Amazon.Com | Barnes & Noble (BN.Com) | Books A Million (BAM.Com)

BOBO's

CHILDREN ACTIVITY BOOKS

COLORING, DRAWING & ACTIVITY BOOKS FOR CHILDREN

Now draw your anything what you want here. It's time to draw your masterpiece!